Dear Teachers and Parents,

Bible Character Codes was designed to give students a better understanding of some of the people found in the Bible.

Beginning with Adam and Eve and ending with Philemon, students and adults will find the character codes an exciting way to learn more about God's people. Different degrees of difficulty make each code a new learning experience—for example, many of the puzzles do not have complete codes. This makes the puzzles challenging for children and adults alike. Children may have fun working on the puzzles together. Adult Bible classes might find the puzzles an interesting change of pace in their lessons. There are *many* ways to use this book.

Challenging Ways to Use Bible Character Codes

1. Photocopy the pages without the code. Place one letter at a time on the chalkboard until someone completes the puzzle.
2. Use your Bible and reference books to discover other interesting facts about the people listed in this book.
3. Use the code given for a particular character to make up your own puzzle about that person.
4. After you have solved a puzzle, use a concordance to discover where in the Bible the verse is located.
5. Have children make up their own secret codes. Have them write short descriptions about themselves. Then photocopy the puzzle for the class or other children to solve. The goal is to discover which classmate the puzzle is about.

Enjoy working these puzzles and coming up with your own Bible character codes!

William Schlegl

"I will be their God, and they will be My people." 2 Corinthians 6:16

Bible Character Codes

William Schlegl

CPH
SAINT LOUIS

Scripture quotations taken from the HOLY BIBLE, NEW INTERNATIONAL VERSION®. NIV®. Copyright © 1973, 1978, 1984 by International Bible Society. Used by permission of Zondervan Publishing House. All rights reserved.

Copyright © 1998 Concordia Publishing House
3558 S. Jefferson Avenue, St. Louis, MO 63118-3968
Manufactured in the United States of America

Teachers and parents may reproduce the activities herein for classroom use or for use in the home. Reproduction for an entire school or school system, or for resale, is prohibited.

All rights reserved. Except as noted above, no part of this publication may be reproduced, stored in a retrieval system, or transmitted, in any form or by any means, electronic, mechanical, photocopying, recording, or otherwise, without the prior written permission of Concordia Publishing House.

1 2 3 4 5 6 7 8 9 10   07 06 05 04 03 02 01 00 99 98

Old Testament Language

The books of the Old Testament were written in Hebrew. Below is a simple version of the Hebrew language. As you translate the Hebrew message, keep in mind that Hebrew is read from right to left.

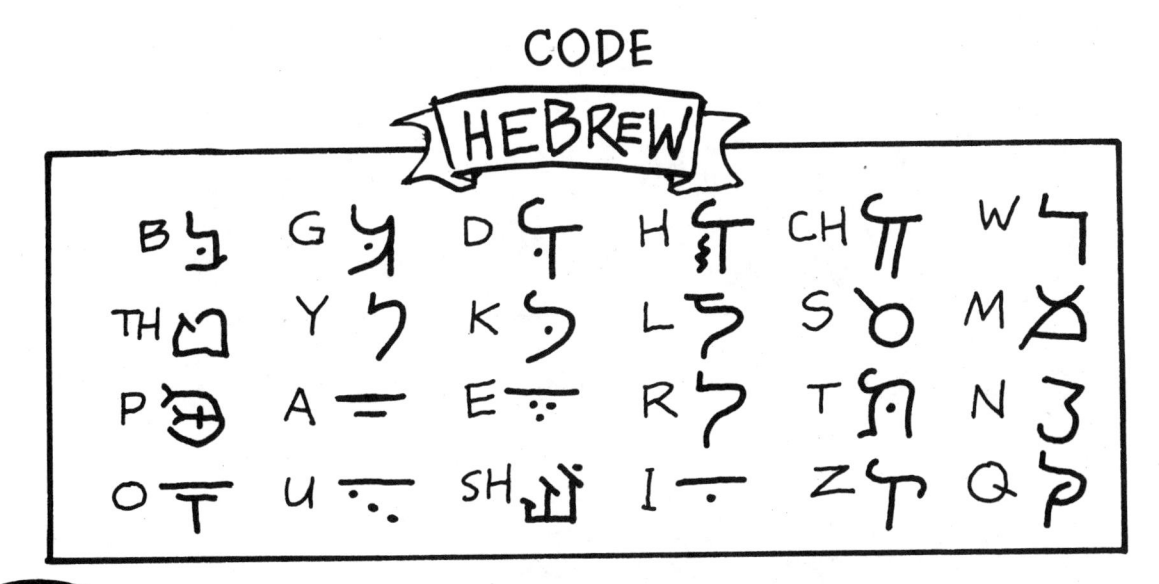

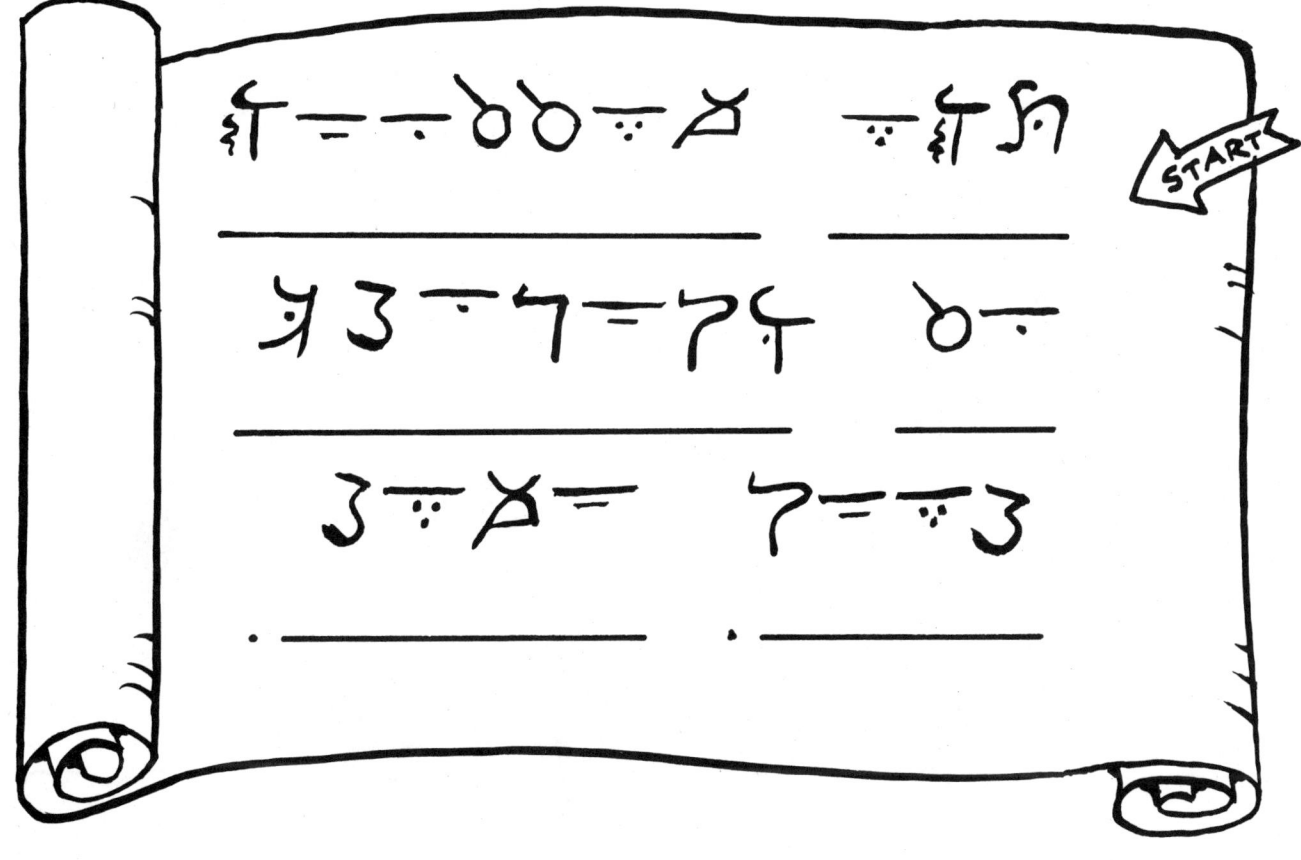

CODE — HEBREW

B	G	D	H	CH	W	
TH	Y	K	L	S	M	
P	A	E	R	T	N	
O	U	SH	I	Z	Q	

Adam and Eve

Adam and Eve were placed in the Garden of Eden to take care of God's wonderful creation. We remember them as the parents of the human race. As the first people, Adam and Eve were blessed in a marvelous way.

CODE

A O C ⊖ D ⊘ E ☺ F ⊕ G ⊘ H ⊘ I ⊗
L ◐ M ● N ◒ O ◓ R ⊖ S ⊟ T ⊡ W ☉

Cain and Abel

Cain and Abel were the children of Adam and Eve. Cain was a farmer, and Abel was a shepherd. Both brought burnt offerings to the Lord, but Abel's offering was accepted over his brother's offering.

Noah

Noah built the ark according to God's specifications. Noah, his wife, his sons, and their wives were all saved from the great flood that covered the earth. After the flood, God blessed Noah and his family and told them to fill the earth. Why was Noah blessed in this special way?

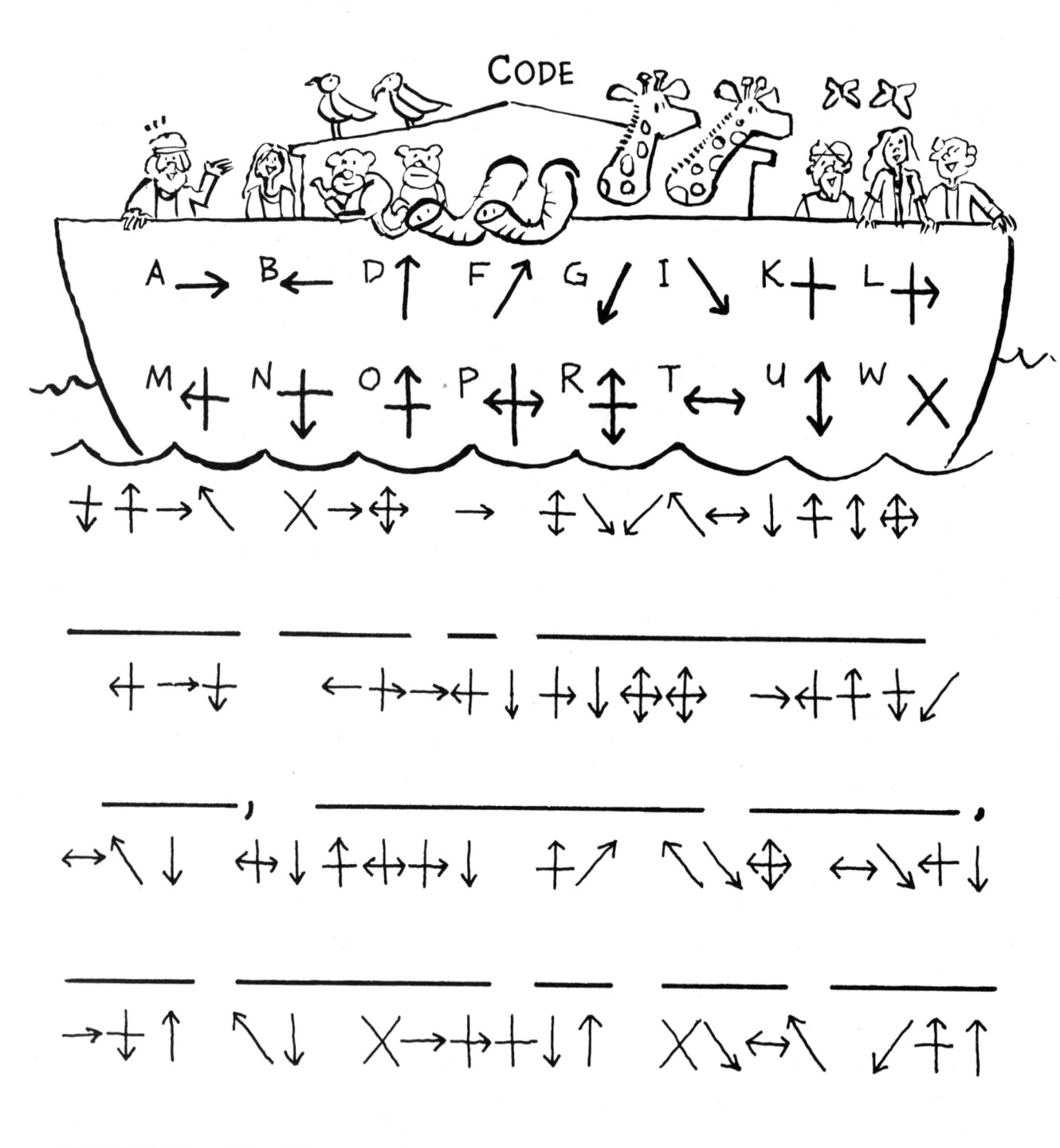

CODE

A →   B ←   D ↑   F ↗   G ↙   I ↘   K ✚   L ⇨
M ⬅   N ⬇   O ⬆   P ⬌   R ↕   T ↔   U ⇩   W   X

Abraham

5

We call Abraham the "patriarch," the father, of the Hebrew people. While Abraham was still childless, God gave him a promise concerning his descendants. Abraham believed God's promise. What was that promise?

CODE

▽	△	◁	▷	∧	∨	⟨	⟩	∪	⊂	⊃	⊐	⌐	⌙	○	d	b	⊓	⊔	∨	⊓
A	B	C	D	E	F	G	H	I	K	L	M	N	O	P	R	S	T	U	V	Y

"_ _ _ _   _ _   _ _   _ _ _   _ _ _ _ _ _

_ _ _   _ _ _ _ _   _ _ _   _ _ _ _ _ _,

_ _   _ _ _ _ _ _   _ _ _   _ _ _   _ _ _ _ _

_ _ _   _ _ _ _   _ _   _ _ _ _   _ _."

_ _ _ _.   "_ _   _ _ _ _ _   _ _ _ _

_ _ _ _ _ _ _ _ _ _   _ _ _ _ _ _."

6

Isaac

Isaac means "laughter." Isaac's elderly mother, Sarah, laughed when she heard that she was going to have a son because she was too old to have children. When Isaac was a boy, what did God ask Abraham to do? Solve the puzzle below.

CODE

# 7

Jacob

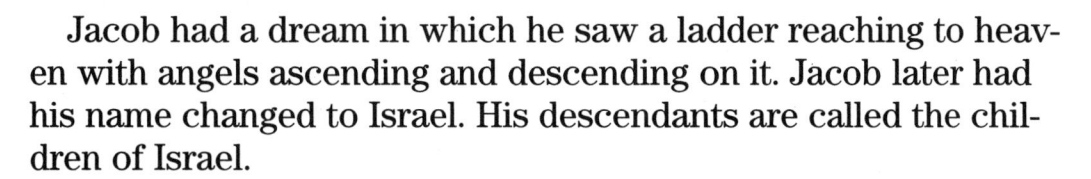

Jacob had a dream in which he saw a ladder reaching to heaven with angels ascending and descending on it. Jacob later had his name changed to Israel. His descendants are called the children of Israel.

Code

8 Joseph

Joseph received a coat of many colors because he was the favorite son of his father, Jacob. Joseph had several dreams that showed he was to be a ruler over his brothers. These dreams became reality years later when Joseph was ruler over Egypt.

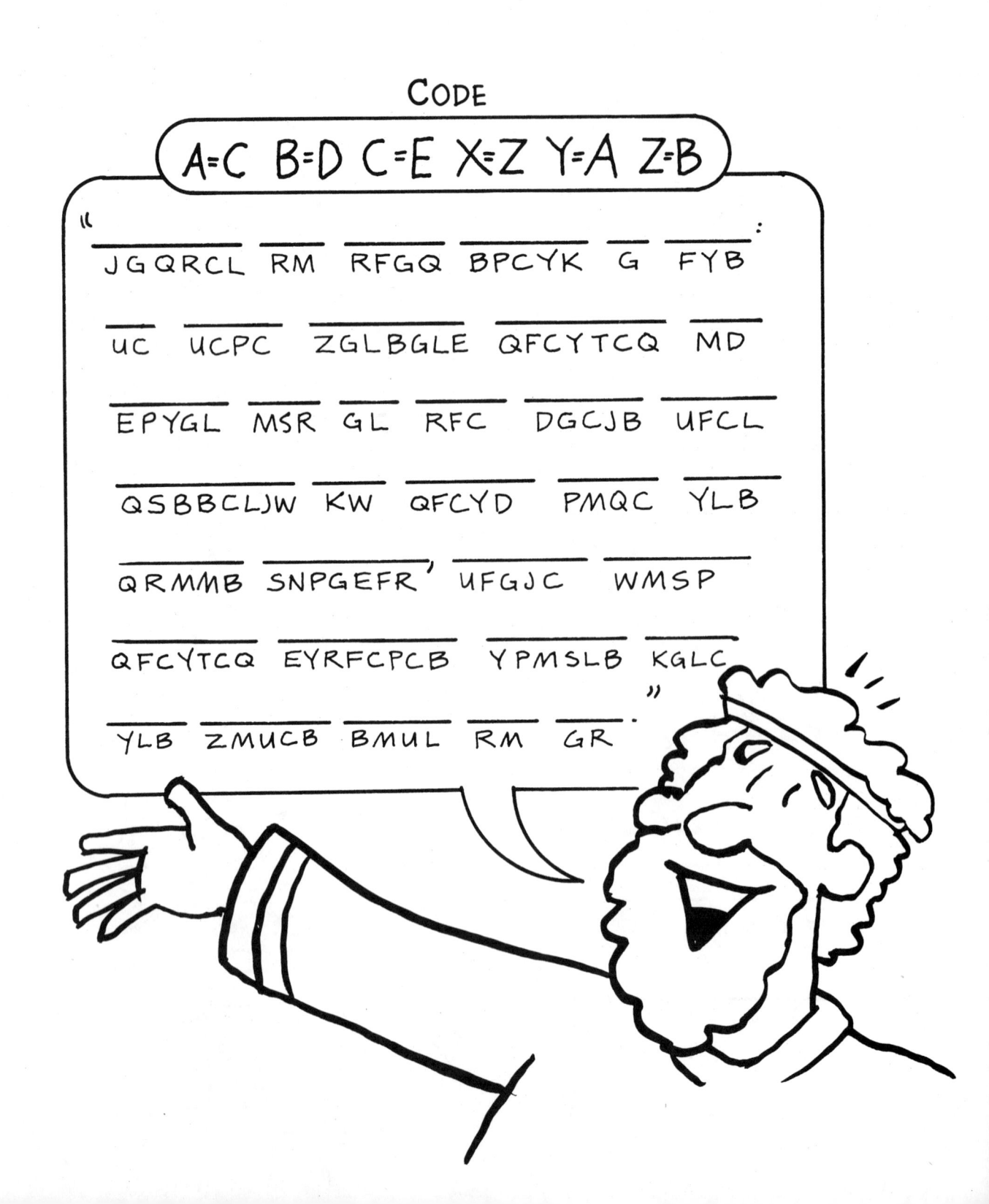

Code

A=C B=D C=E X=Z Y=A Z=B

"_____ __ ____ _____ _ ___
 JGQRCL RM RFGQ BPCYK G FYB

__ ____ _____ _____ __
UC UCPC ZGLBGLE QFCYTCQ MD

_____ ___ __ ___ _____ ____
EPYGL MSR GL RFC DGCJB UFCL

_____ __ _____ ____ ___
QSBBCLJW KW QFCYD PMQC YLB

_____ _____' _____ ____
QRMMB SNPGEFR UFGJC WMSP

_____ _____ _____ ____
QFCYTCQ EYRFCPCB YPMSLB KGLC
"
___ _____ ____ __ __.
YLB ZMUCB BMUL RM GR

Moses

Moses led the children of Israel out of Egypt toward the Promised Land. Moses went to the top of Mount Sinai to receive the commandments of the Lord. What a privilege it must have been to speak directly to the Lord.

9

CODE

A=1 E=5 I=9 O=15 U=21

23 8 5 14 — 20 8 5 — 12 15 18 4 — 6 9 14 9 19 8 5 4
__ __ __ __   __ __ __   __ __ __ __   __ __ __ __ __ __ __

19 16 5 1 11 9 14 7 — 20 15 — 13 15 19 5 19 — 15 14
__ __ __ __ __ __ __ __   __ __   __ __ __ __ __   __ __

13 15 21 14 20 — 19 9 14 1 9 — 8 5 — 7 1 22 5 — 8 9 13
__ __ __ __ __   __ __ __ __ __   __ __   __ __ __ __ __   __ __ __ ,

20 8 5 — 20 23 15 — 20 1 2 12 5 20 19 — 15 6 — 20 8 5
__ __ __   __ __ __   __ __ __ __ __ __ __   __ __   __ __ __

20 5 19 20 9 13 15 14 25 — 20 8 5 — 20 1 2 12 5 20 19 — 15 6
__ __ __ __ __ __ __ __ __   __ __ __   __ __ __ __ __ __ __   __ __ ,

19 20 15 14 5 — 9 14 19 3 18 9 2 5 4 — 2 25 — 20 8 5
__ __ __ __ __   __ __ __ __ __ __ __ __ __   __ __   __ __ __

6 9 14 7 5 18 — 15 6 — 7 15 4
__ __ __ __ __ __   __ __   __ __ __ .

10 Aaron

Aaron was the spokesman for his brother, Moses, before the mighty Pharaoh. He helped the Israelites defeat the Amalekites by holding up Moses' arms. Aaron became the first high priest of Israel.

Joshua

11

Joshua was one of two spies who gave an encouraging report on the conquest of the land of Canaan. He became the leader of the Israelites after the death of Moses. Joshua led the children of Israel into the Promised Land and followed the commands of God throughout his life.

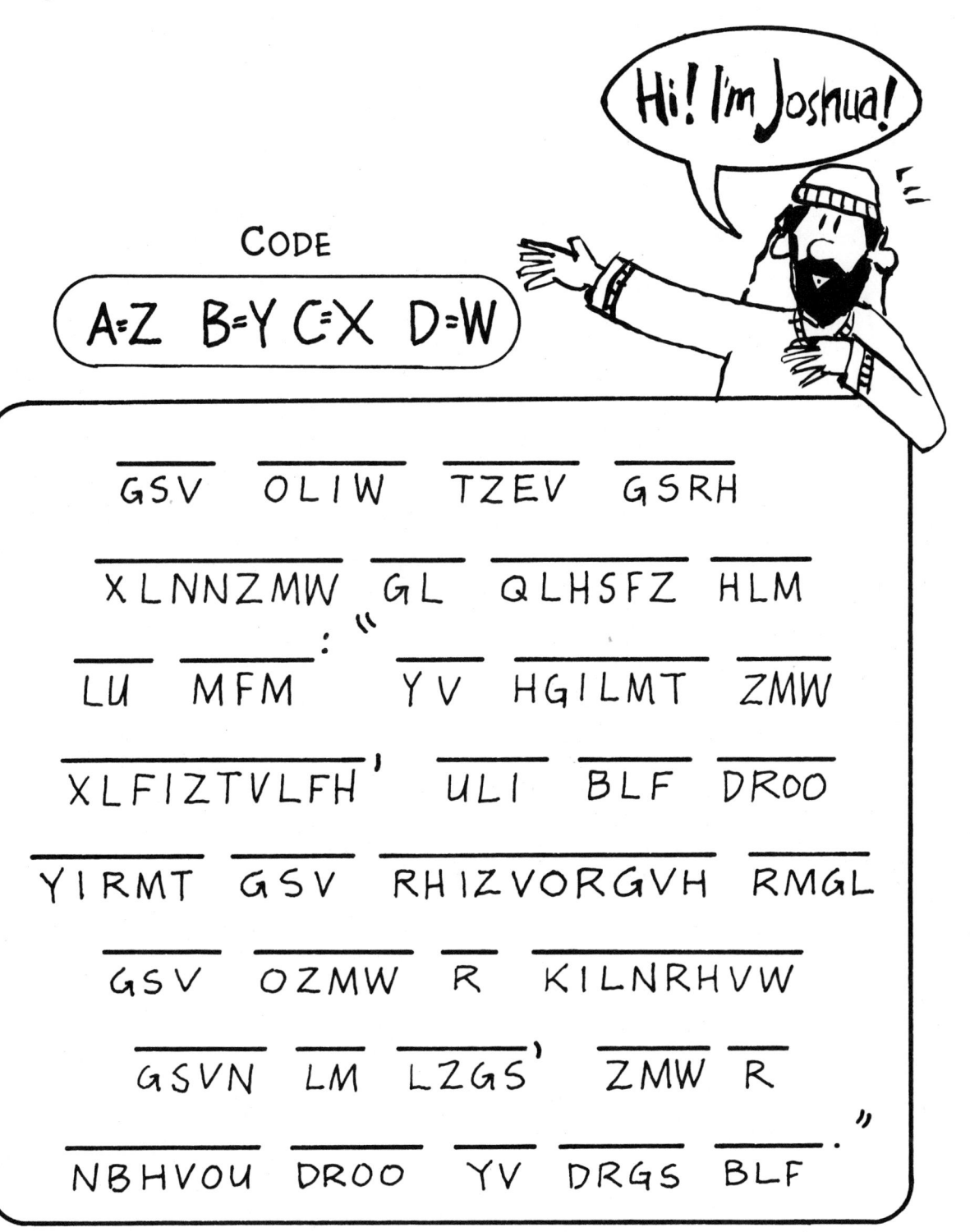

Hi! I'm Joshua!

Code
A=Z B=Y C=X D=W

GSV OLIW TZEV GSRH XLNNZMW GL QLHSFZ HLM LU MFM: "YV HGILMT ZMW XLFIZTVLFH, ULI BLF DROO YIRMT GSV RHIZVORGVH RMGL GSV OZMW R KILNRHVW GSVN LM LZGS' ZMW R NBHVOU DROO YV DRGS BLF."

(The lord gave this command to Joshua son of Nun: "Be strong and courageous, for you will bring the Israelites into the land I promised them on oath, and I myself will be with you.")

Job

Job, a man of great patience, feared the Lord. Even after losing all his worldly possessions and suffering a terrible sickness, Job still loved the Lord. Solve the puzzle below to see what Job said about God.

Deborah

13

Deborah was a prophetess and a leader of Israel. The land of Israel had been oppressed for 20 years, and the people went to Deborah for help. She assembled an army and with the help of God defeated the enemy.

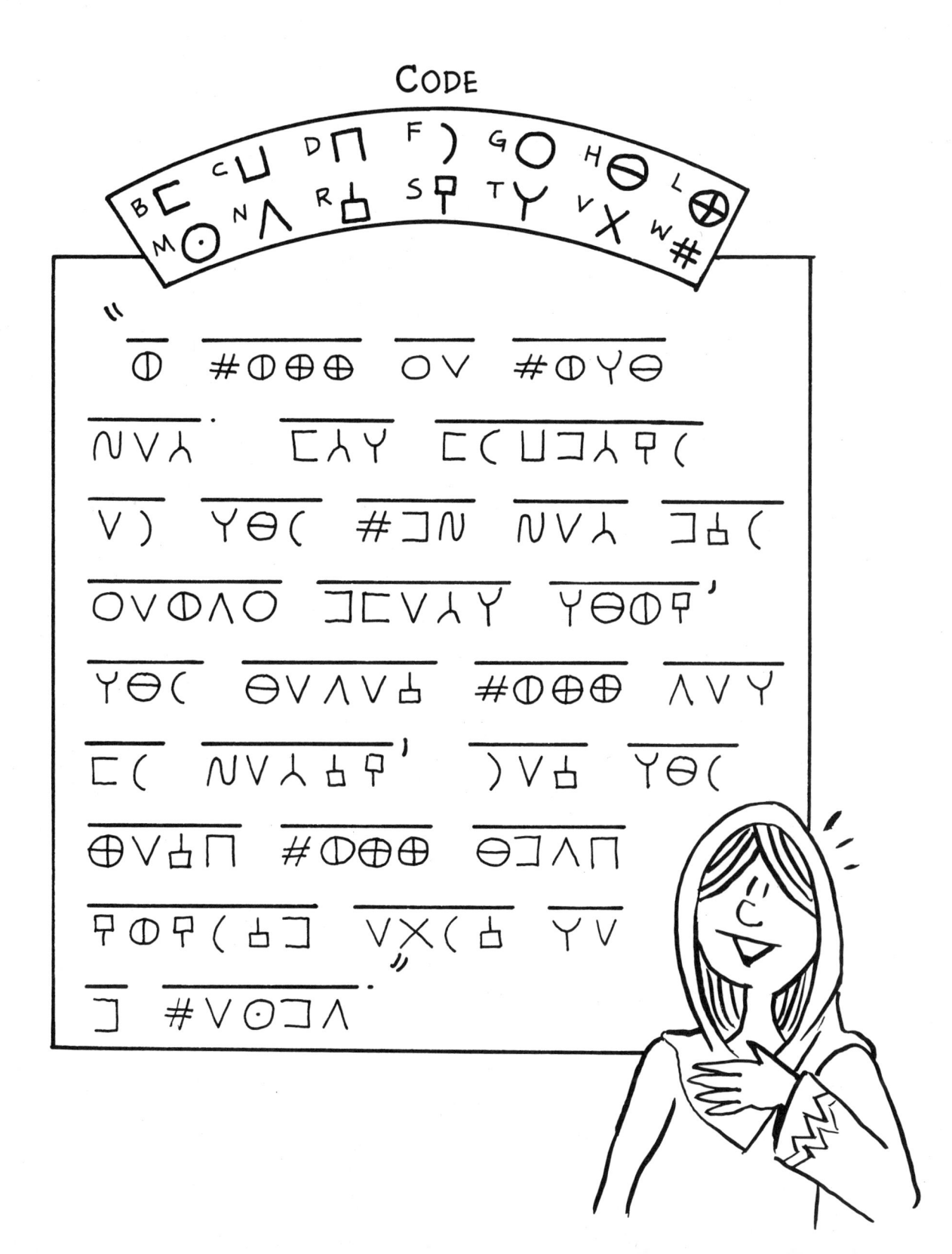

Code

[Cipher puzzle]

Gideon

14

Gideon was chosen by God to lead the Israelites against their enemy. Out of thousands of men who wanted to fight with him, Gideon chose only 300. This showed the people that it was God who was delivering them, not their own power. Gideon used a strange battle tactic for the victory. Read about it in the puzzle below.

CODE

A=X̤ D=X̤ E=Ẍ H=X̤
I=X̤ O=+ R=+̤ T=+ U=+̤

(Decoded solution:)

HE DIVIDED THE THREE

__ __   __ __ __ __ __ __   __ __ __ __ __ __

HUNDRED MEN INTO THREE

__ __ __ __ __ __ __   __ __ __   __ __ __ __ __

COMPANIES AND HE

__ __ __ __ __ __ __ __ __   __ __ __   __ __

PUT A TRUMPET IN EVERY

__ __ __   __   __ __ __ __ __ __ __   __ __   __ __ __ __ __

"A TORCH AND A TRUMPET,

__   __ __ __ __ __   __ __ __   __   __ __ __ __ __ __ __,

IN EVERY MAN'S HAND, AND

__ __   __ __ __ __ __   __ __ __   __ __ __   __ __ __ __,

THEY CRIED."

__ __ __ __   __ __ __   __ __ __ __ __ __.

Samson

15

Samson was a man of exceptional strength. He used his great strength to fight the Philistines, the enemy of the children of Israel. What made Samson different?

Code

Z=01 A=02 Y=03 B=04

16

Ruth

Ruth was a Moabite woman who returned with her mother-in-law, Naomi, to the land of Judah. She gleaned wheat in the fields and later married Boaz. Read her words of devotion to Naomi in the puzzle below.

Code

B D G H L M N P R S T W Y

"Whither thou goest, I will go; and where thou lodgest, I will lodge: thy people shall be my people, and thy God my God."

Samuel

17

Samuel was a prophet whose mother had promised him to the Lord before he was born. It was Samuel who anointed the first two kings of Israel. He constantly urged the people to follow the Lord.

"_ _____ _____ _____
_____ _____ _____
_____ _____ _____
_____ _____ _____.
_____ _____ _____
_____ _____ _____
_____ _____
_____ _____ _____."

18

Saul

Saul was the first king of Israel. He ruled for 40 years. His deliberate disobedience caused God to reject him as king. Saul died in disgrace.

Code

David

David was the shepherd boy who defeated the Philistine giant, Goliath. Goliath was heavily armed, while David only had a sling and some small stones. How was David able to achieve this amazing victory?

CODE

(code wheel shown)

"_____ _____
_____ _____
_____ _____
_____ _____ _____
_____ _____ _____ _____
_____ _____,_____ _____
_____ _____ _____
_____ _____
_____"

20 Solomon

Solomon, the third king of Israel, was blessed with great wisdom. His fame spread, and people of all nations came to listen to Solomon's teachings. The Lord gave great wisdom to Solomon because of his humble request for guidance.

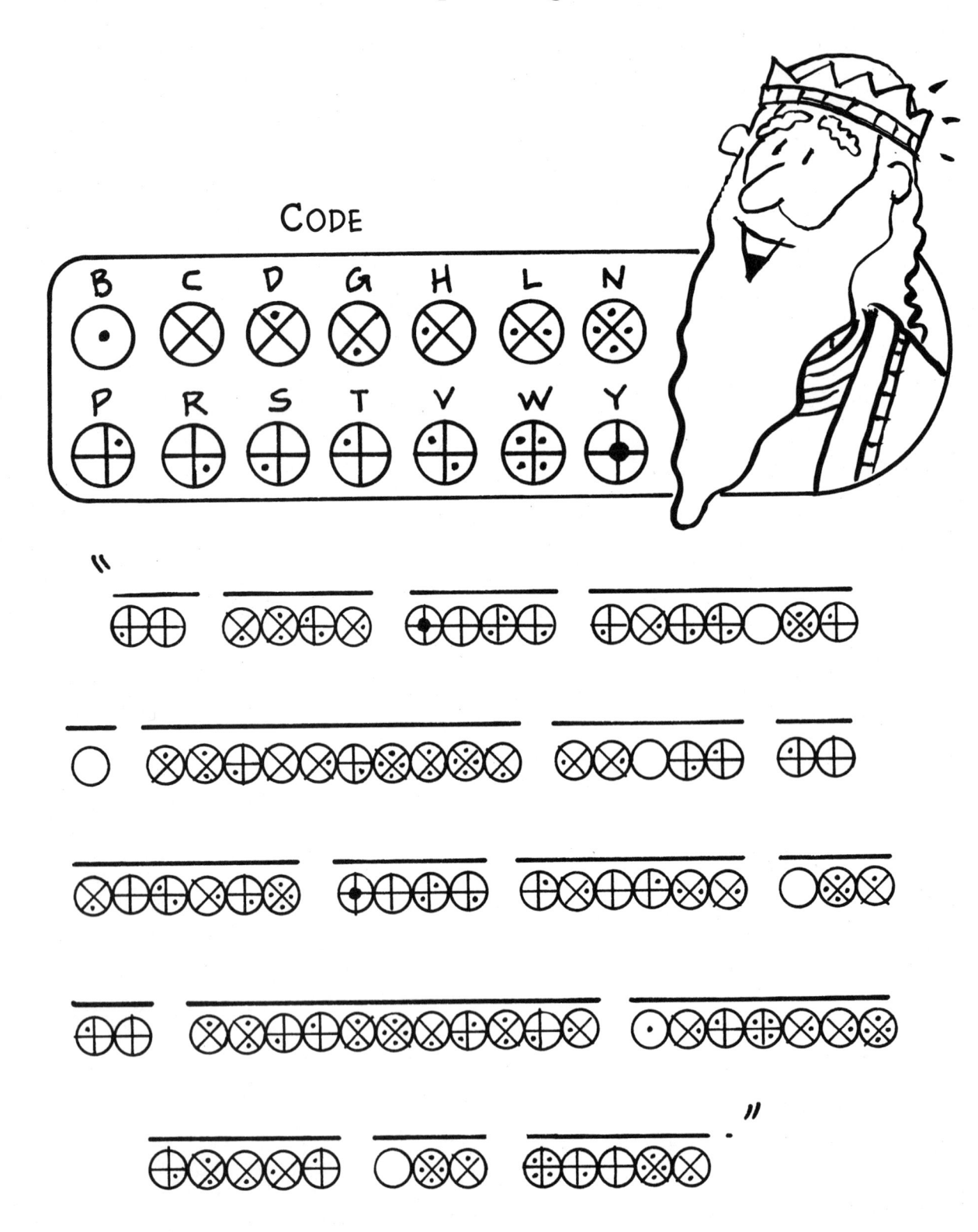

CODE

B C D G H L N
P R S T V W Y

Elijah

21

Elijah prophesied that a famine would come upon the land of Israel. This famine was the result of the Israelites' worshiping false gods instead of the one true God. The Lord provided for Elijah and later took him to heaven in a fiery chariot.

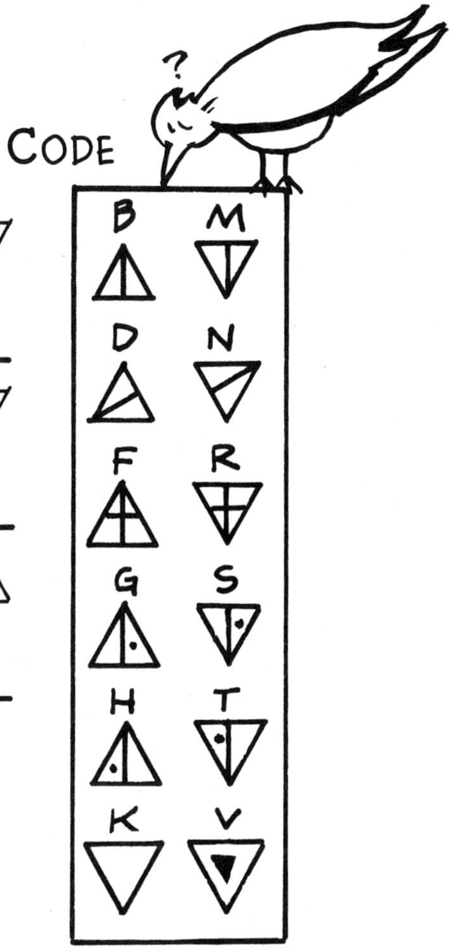

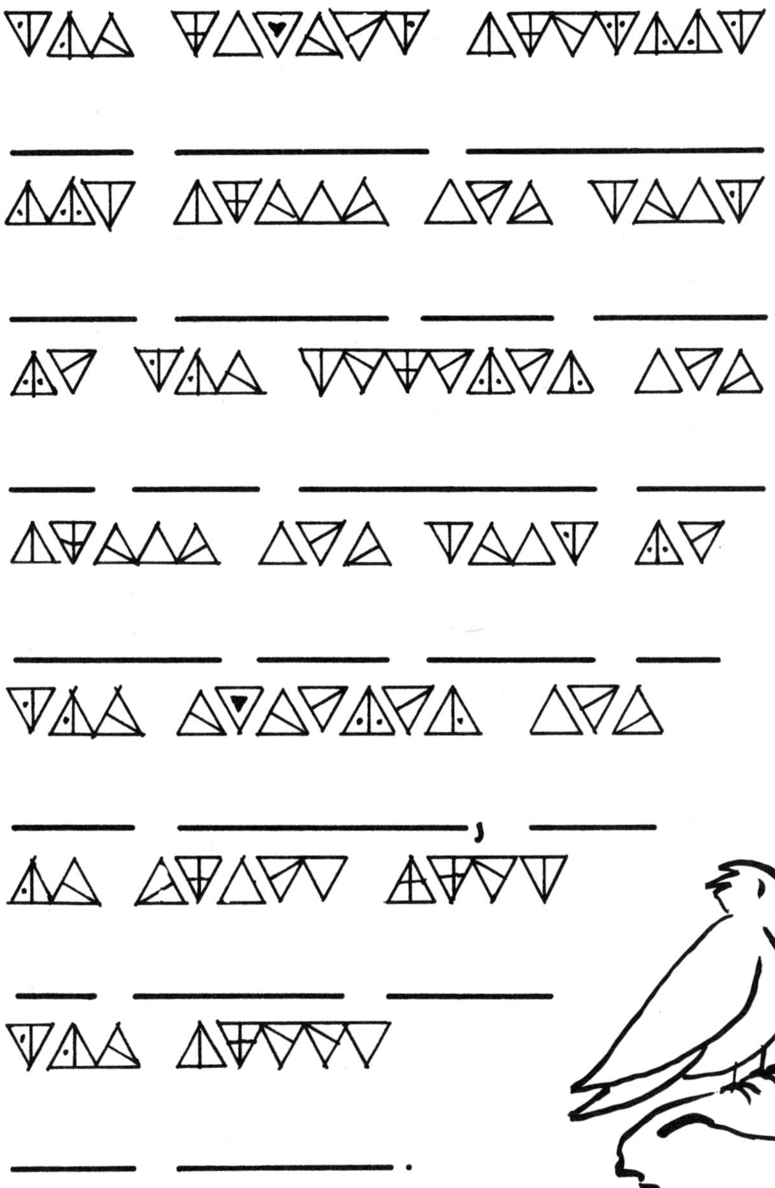

Elisha

Elisha received the mantle from his teacher, Elijah. Elisha performed many miracles of kindness and mercy. With God's help, Elisha healed the leprosy of Naaman, a commander of the Syrian army.

"Go, wash yourself seven times in the Jordan, and your flesh will be restored and you will be cleansed."

Esther

Esther was a beautiful Jewish girl who became queen of Persia. Risking her own life, Esther appealed to the king and saved her people from massacre. This rescue was the origin of the Feast of Purim, which Jewish people still observe today.

23

24

Jonah

God told Jonah to go to the wicked city of Nineveh, but Jonah ran away. He was swallowed by a great fish and spent three days and nights inside the fish. Jonah repented of his wickedness, and the fish deposited him on dry land. Jonah then carried out God's mission to Nineveh.

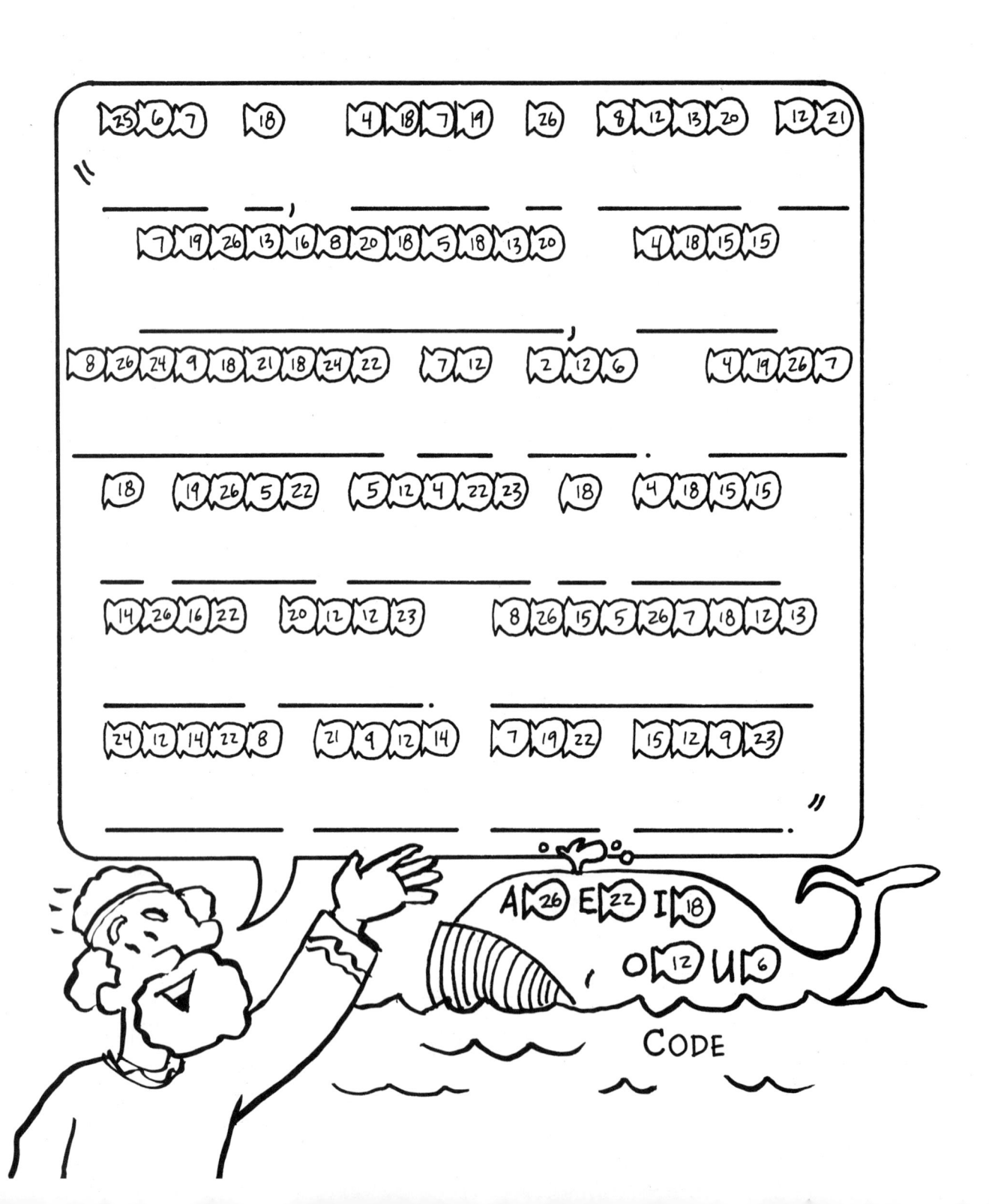

"___ ___, ___ ___ ___ ___ ___ ___ ___ ___ ___ ___
 25 6 7   18   4 18 7 19   26   8 12 13 20   12 21

___ ___ ___ ___ ___ ___ ___ ___ ___ ___ ___   ___ ___ ___ ___
 7 19 26 13 16 8 20 18 5 18 13 20   4 18 15 15

___ ___ ___ ___ ___ ___ ___ ___   ___ ___   ___ ___ ___   ___ ___ ___ ___.
 8 26 24 9 18 21 18 24 22   7 12   2 12 6   4 19 26 7

___ ___   ___ ___ ___ ___   ___ ___ ___ ___ ___   ___ ___   ___ ___ ___ ___
 18   19 26 5 22   5 12 4 22 23   18   4 18 15 15

___ ___ ___ ___   ___ ___ ___ ___   ___ ___ ___ ___ ___ ___ ___ ___ ___
 14 26 16 22   20 12 12 23   8 26 15 5 26 7 18 12 13

___ ___ ___ ___ ___   ___ ___ ___ ___   ___ ___ ___   ___ ___ ___ ___."
 24 12 14 22 8   21 9 12 14   7 19 22   15 12 9 23

CODE: A=26 E=22 I=18 O=12 U=6

Isaiah

Isaiah was called the messianic prophet because of his many prophecies concerning the coming Messiah. He was a great writer and is quoted in the New Testament more than any other prophet.

25

Code

B	C	D	F
G	H	L	M
N	P	R	S
T	V	W	Y

Puzzle: decode the cipher.

26 Jeremiah

Jeremiah was called by God to warn Judah about its wickedness. He was placed into an old cistern below the prison floor. God saved Jeremiah from the well, and he continued to preach the destruction of Jerusalem.

"_ _ _ _ _ _ _ _ _ _ _ _ _ _ _ _ _ _ _

_ _ _ _ _ _ _ _ _ _ _ _ _ _ _ _

_ _ _ _ _ _ _ _ _ _ _ _ _ _ _ _ _ _ _,

_ _ _ _ _ _ _ _ _ _ _ _; _ _ _ _ _ _ _ _ _ _ _ _ _ _

_ _ _ _ _ _ _ _ _

_ _ _ _ _ _ _ _ _ _."

Ezekiel

Ezekiel was a prophet to God's people while they were in exile in Babylon. He explained why God allowed this punishment to come to His people. The Lord took Ezekiel to the valley of dry bones and made them living beings. What lesson was God teaching Ezekiel and His people?

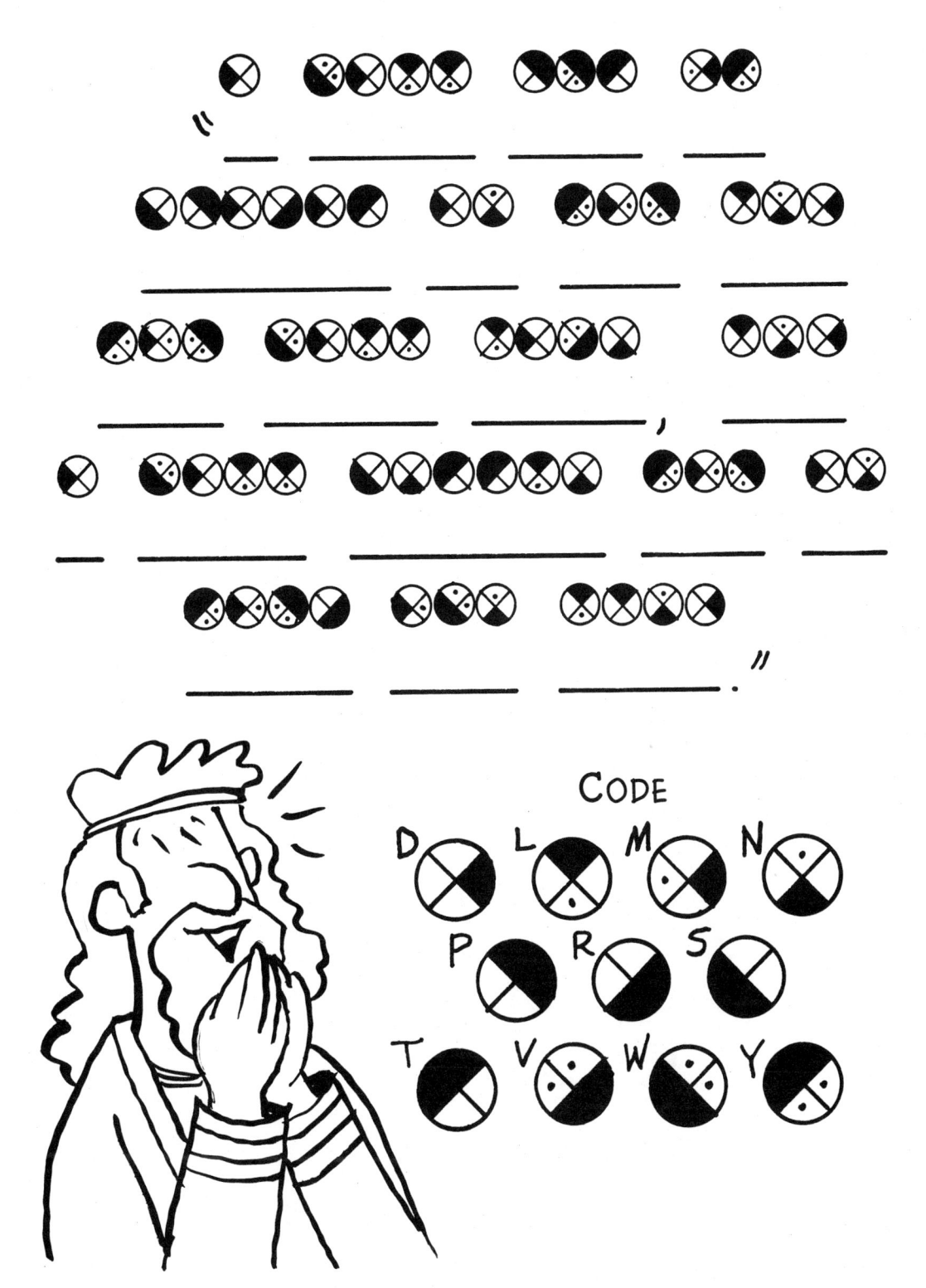

"I will put my Spirit in you and you will live and I will place you in your own land."

28 Daniel

Daniel was a very religious man who rose to great power in Babylonia. He lived in a land of idol worship, but he remained firm in his faith in the one true God. The Lord protected Daniel when he was placed in the lions' den. Why was Daniel protected?

"_ _   _ _ _   _ _ _   _ _ _   ' _ _ _ _ _   _ _,
 M Y   G O D   H A S   S E N T   H I S

 _ _   _ _ _   _ _ _   _ _ _ _ _   _ _   _ _ _
 A N   G E L   A N D   S H U T   T H   E L I ...

(ANGEL AND SHUT THE LIONS' MOUTHS. THEY HAVE NOT HURT ME, FOR I WAS FOUND INNOCENT IN HIS SIGHT.)

Shadrach, Meshach, and Abednego

29

Shadrach, Meshach, and Abednego were Hebrew men who were appointed administrators over the province of Babylon. They refused to bow down to a golden idol, and the king had them thrown into a fiery furnace. But they were not harmed at all. Why did the fire not harm Shadrach, Meshach, and Abednego?

CODE

B C D F G H K L
M N R S T U W Z

30 New Testament Language

The books of the New Testament were written in Greek, the language commonly spoken at the time of the apostles. Below is a simple version of the Greek alphabet. Translate the Greek message.

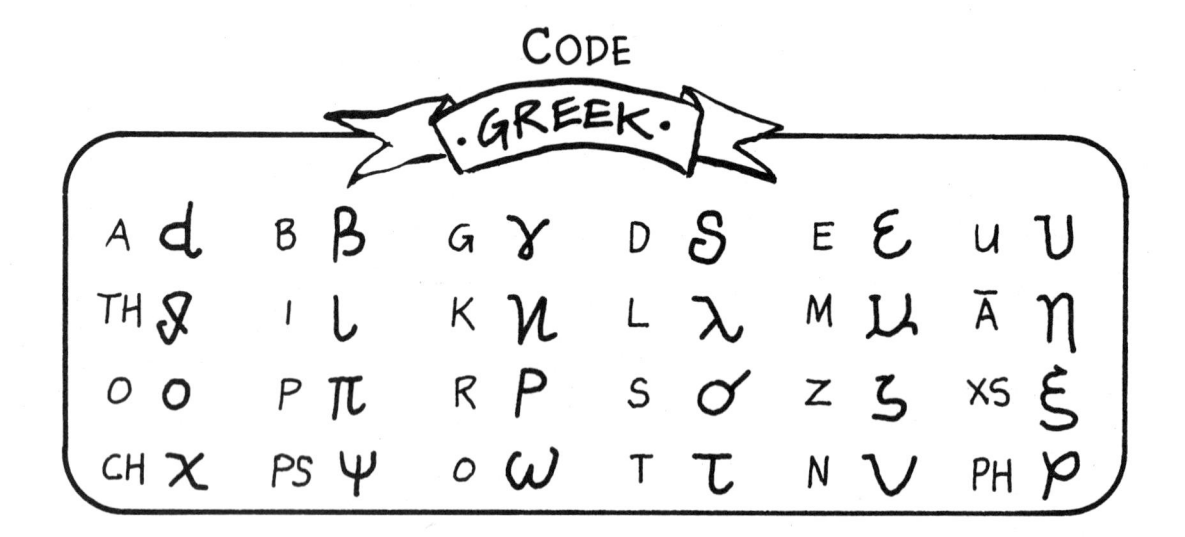

CODE: GREEK

A	α	B	β	G	γ	D	δ	E	ε	U	υ
TH	ϑ	I	ι	K	κ	L	λ	M	μ	Ā	η
O	o	P	π	R	ρ	S	σ	Z	ζ	XS	ξ
CH	χ	PS	ψ	O	ω	T	τ	N	ν	PH	ρ

σεεν ϑε λoρs

_____ _____ _____

(SEEN THE LORD)

Peter

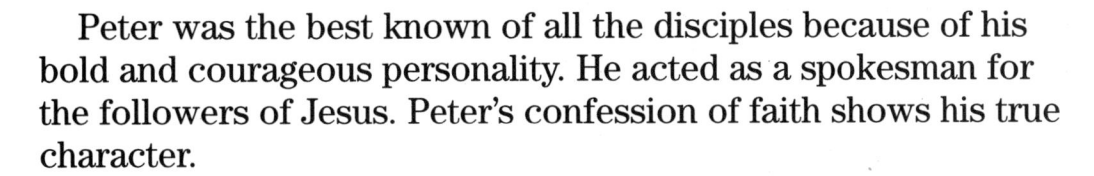

31

Peter was the best known of all the disciples because of his bold and courageous personality. He acted as a spokesman for the followers of Jesus. Peter's confession of faith shows his true character.

"___ ___ ___, ___ ___ ___ ___ ___ ___ ___ ___ ___ ___?" ... ___ ___ ___ ___ ___ ___ ___ "___ ___ ___, ___ ___ ___ ___ ___ ___ ___."

32 Andrew

Andrew was the first of the disciples to know Jesus. He is known as the first Christian missionary because he brought his brother, Peter, to Jesus.

Code

A	B	C	E	F	G	I
L	M	O	R	S	U	V

The one whose first number two

___ _____ _____ _____ ___

one to meet the Messiah

___ __ ____ ___ _____

Jesus was Andrew his is own

_____ ___ ____ ___ __ ___

brother Simon, "We have

_____ ___ _____," __ ____

found the Messiah" (____ __,

_____ ___ _____

the Christ

__ ____).

James

James, the brother of John, was one of the first four disciples called by Jesus. Several stories in the Bible characterize James as having great devotion to Jesus' work. James was the first disciple to be martyred.

33

CODE

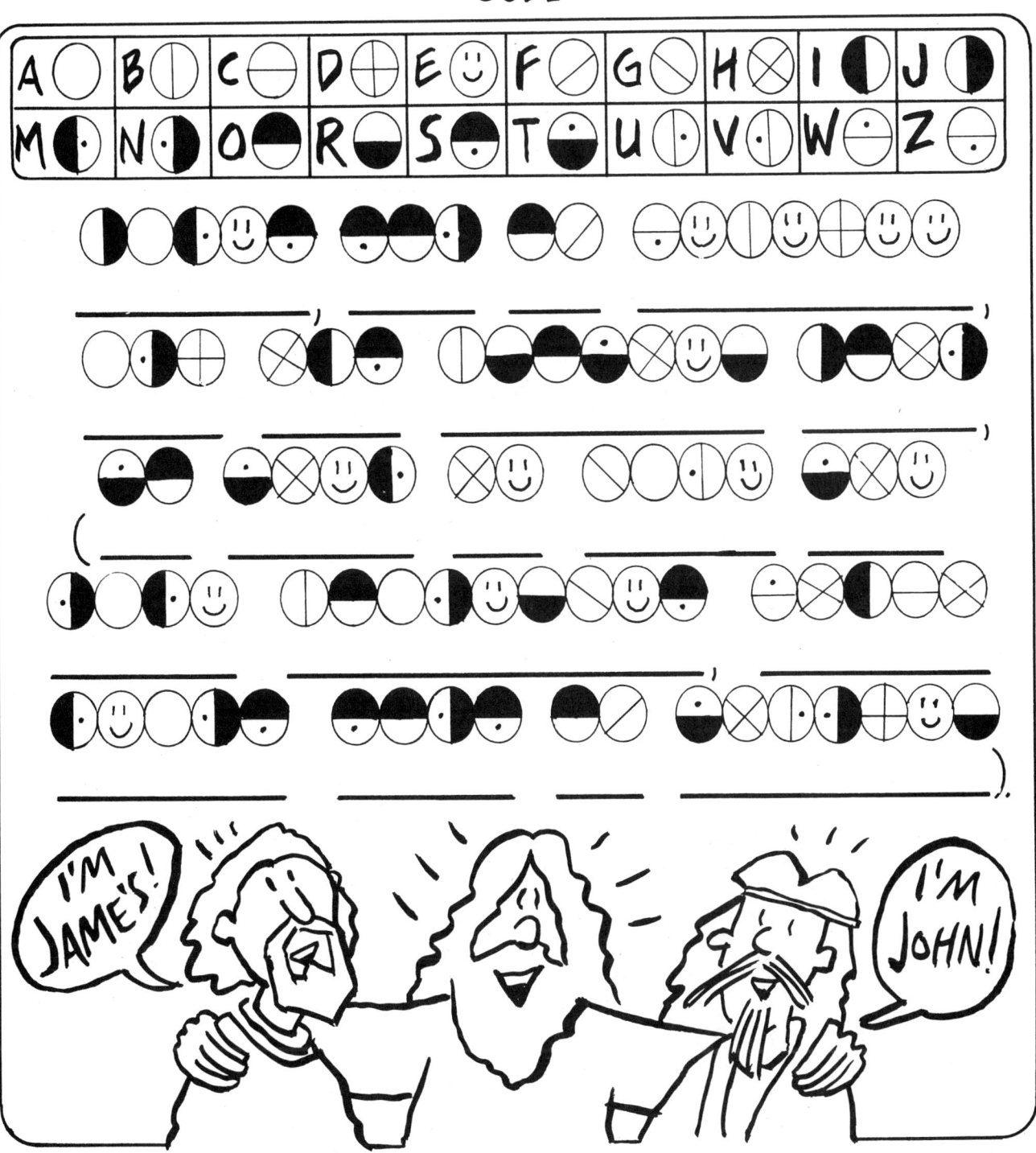

A	B	C	D	E	F	G	H	I	J
M	N	O	R	S	T	U	V	W	Z

Solve the code to reveal the message.

34

John

John is often called the "beloved disciple." He had a strong desire to share the love of Jesus with all people. He used the word *love* more than 50 times in his first epistle.

CODE

A ↑	B ↓	C →	E ↕	F ↔
G ↗	I ↖	L ↙	N +	O ↥
R ↦	T ⊣	U ↨	V ⟷	

Philip

35

Upon accepting Jesus' call, Philip found Nathanael and brought him to the Savior. Philip became the second Christian missionary.

___PHILIP___ ___FOUND___ ___NATHANAEL___ ___AND___
KSRORK ULFMW MZGSZMZVO ZMW

"___TOLD___ ___HIM___,' ___WE___ ___HAVE___ ___FOUND___ ___THE___ ___ONE___
GLOW SRN' DV SZEV ULFMW GSV LMV

___MOSES___ ___WROTE___ ___ABOUT___ ___IN___ ___THE___ ___LAW___,'
NLHVH DILGV ZYLFG RM GSV OZD

___AND___ ___ABOUT___ ___WHOM___ ___THE___ ___PROPHETS___
ZMW ZYLFG DSLN GSV KILKSVGH

___ALSO___ ___WROTE___ ___JESUS___ ___OF___ ___NAZARETH___,
ZOHL DILGV QVHFH LU MZAZIVGS

___THE___ ___SON___ ___OF___ ___JOSEPH___."
GSV HLM LU QLHVKS

CODE: A=Z B=Y C=X D=W

36

Nathanael

Nathanael's surname was Bartholomew. He was brought to Jesus by his friend Philip. Jesus welcomed him and showed His divine power by telling Nathanael that He saw him while he was still under the fig tree, before Philip called him. Jesus referred to Nathanael as a wholly honest man.

Thomas

37

Thomas was called the "doubter" because he often hesitated or doubted other people's statements. For Thomas, seeing was believing. Jesus told him that people who have not seen and yet believe are blessed.

Matthew

Matthew, or Levi, was a tax collector for the Roman government. He was probably very wealthy. When Jesus approached Matthew at the tax booth and said, "Follow Me," Matthew left everything and followed Jesus. What an example for all Christians today!

Code

A	B	D	E	G	H	J
L	N	O	R	S	U	W

__As__ __Jesus__ __went__ __on__ __from__

__there__ __he__ __saw__ __a__ __man__ __named__

__Matthew__ __sitting__ __at__ __the__

__tax__ __collector's__ __booth__.

"__Follow__ __me__," __he__

__told__ __him__, __and__

__Matthew__ __got__ __up__

__and__ __followed__ __him__.

Thaddaeus

39

Thaddaeus was also known as Judas, son of James. He is an obscure disciple, speaking only once in the New Testament. Thaddaeus is supposed to have been a great traveler overseas in his work for Christ.

40 Simon

Simon the Zealot is mentioned in the Scriptures only by name. The Zealots were a group of Jewish patriots who were opposed to the Romans ruling their land. Simon wanted Jesus to help them overthrow the Roman rule, but the power of Jesus turned Simon the Zealot into Simon the apostle of God's love.

Judas Iscariot

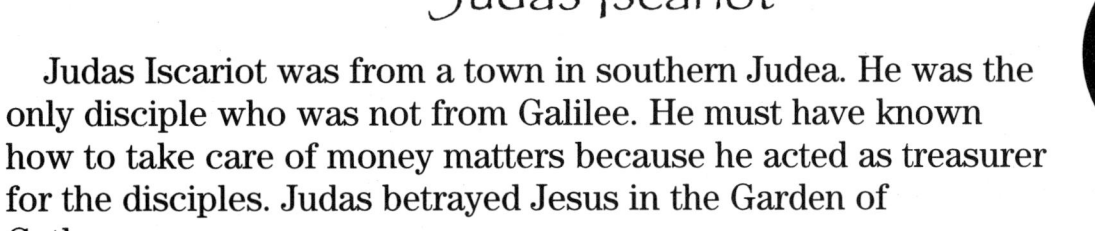

41

Judas Iscariot was from a town in southern Judea. He was the only disciple who was not from Galilee. He must have known how to take care of money matters because he acted as treasurer for the disciples. Judas betrayed Jesus in the Garden of Gethsemane.

"_ _ _ _ _ _ _ _ _ _ _ _," _ _ _ _ _ _ _,
 9 8 1 22 5 19 9 14 14 5 4   8 5 19 1 9 4

"_ _ _ _ _ _ _ _ _ _ _ _ _ _ _ _ _ _ _ _ _ _ _ _
 6 15 18 9 8 1 22 5 2 5 20 18 1 25 5 4 9 14 14 15 3 5 14 20

_ _ _ _ _ _." ... _ _ _ _ _ _ _ _ _ _ _ _ _ _ _
 2 12 15 15 4   19 15 10 21 4 1 19 20 8 18 5 23 20 8 5

_ _ _ _ _ _ _ _ _ _ _ _ _ _ _ _ _ _ _ _ _ _ _ _ _
13 15 14 5 25 9 14 20 15 20 8 5 20 5 13 16 12 5   1 14 4

_ _ _ _ _. _ _ _ _ _ _ _ _ _ _ _ _ _ _
12 5 6 20   20 8 5 14   8 5   23 5 14 20   1 23 1 25

_ _ _ _ _ _ _ _ _ _ _ _ _ _ _ _ _.
1 14 4   8 1 14 7 5 4   8 9 13 19 5 12 6

CODE

A=1 E=5 I=9
O=15 U=21

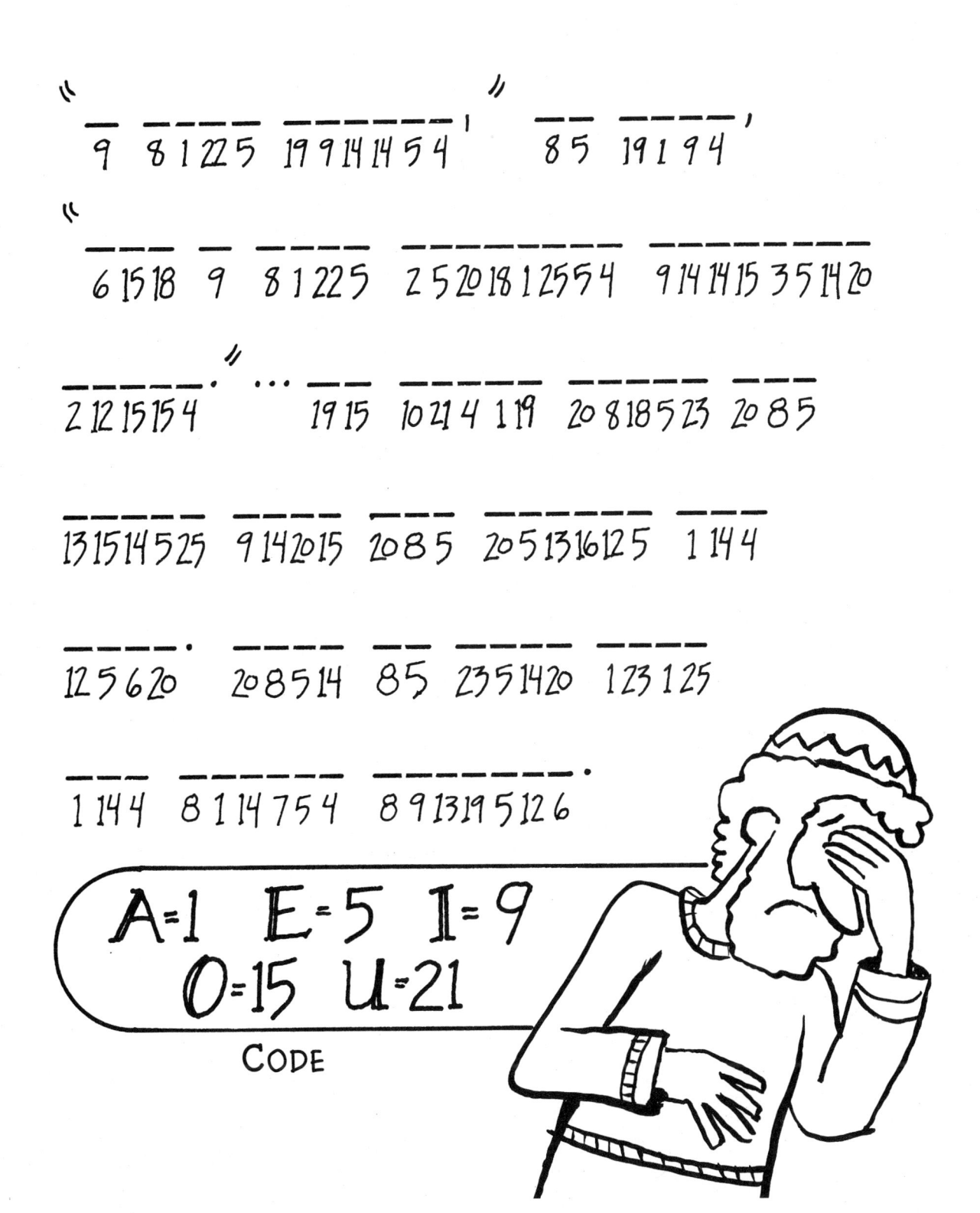

42

Zechariah

Zechariah was a descendant of Aaron who served as a priest in the temple. The angel Gabriel appeared to Zechariah to announce that he would have a son who would be a forerunner to the promised Messiah. Zechariah's promised son was John the Baptist.

___ ___ ___ ___ ___

___ ___ ___ ___ ___

___ ___ ___ ___ ___

___ ___ ___ ___ ,

___ ___ ___ ___ .

CODE

| B | C | E | H | K | L |
| O | R | S | U | V | Y |

John the Baptist

The angel Gabriel foretold that John the Baptist would be filled with the Holy Spirit, even from birth. His mother, Elizabeth, was a cousin of Mary, the mother of Jesus. John lived in the desert until he began preaching to the people of Jerusalem and Judea.

"H AZOSHYD XNT VHSG VZSDQ ATS NMD LNQD ONVDQETK SGZM H VHKK BNLD' SGD SGNMFR NE VGNRD RZMCZKR H ZL MNS VNQSGX SN TMSHD. GD VHKK AZOSHYD XNT VHSG SGD GNKX ROHQHS ZMC VHSG EHQD."

Code: A=B B=C C=D D=E E=F F=G

44

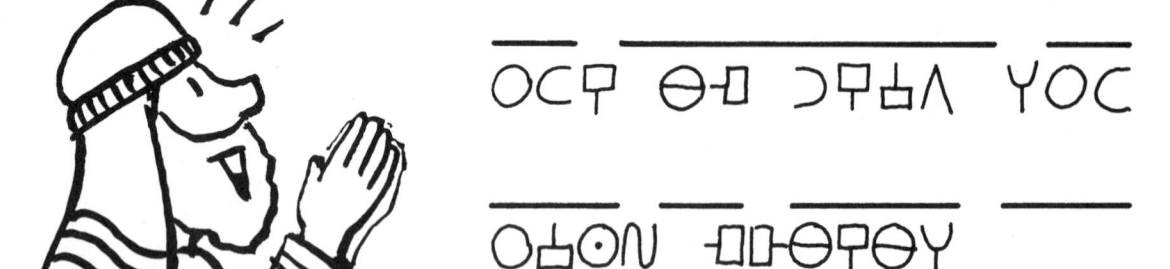

Joseph

Joseph, a descendant of King David, was the husband of Mary, the mother of Jesus. Joseph was a righteous man who followed the teachings of the Lord. An angel appeared to Joseph in a dream and told him that Mary's son would be the Messiah, the promised Savior.

Code

B	C	D	F	H	I	J	K
L	M	N	O	P	R	T	V	X

"_ _ _ _ _ _ _ _ _ _ _ _ _ _ _ _ _ _ _,

_ _ _ _ _ _ _ _ _ _ _ _ _ _ _ _ _ _ _ _ _

_ _ _ _ _ _ _ _ _ _ _ _ _ _ _ _ _ _ _ _,

_ _ _ _ _ _ _ _ _ _ _ _ _

_ _ _ _ _ _ _ _ _ _ _ _

_ _ _ _ _ _ _ _ _ _

_ _ _ _ _."

Mary

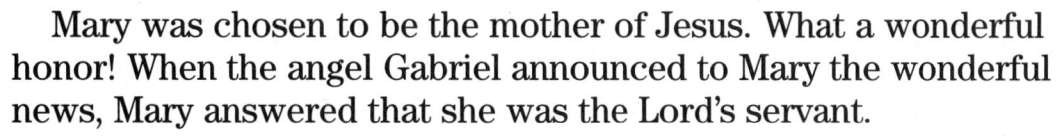

Mary was chosen to be the mother of Jesus. What a wonderful honor! When the angel Gabriel announced to Mary the wonderful news, Mary answered that she was the Lord's servant.

45

CODE

B C D F G H J L M N R S V W

"_ _ _ _ _ _ _ _,_ _ _,
_ _.
_ _ _ _ _ _ _ _ _ _ _ _ _ _ _ _ _ _ _
_ _ _ _ _ _ _ _ _ _ _ _ _,
_ _ _ _ _ _ _ _ _ _ _ _ _."

Jesus Christ

46

Jesus is the Savior of the world. It is only through the perfect life, death, and resurrection of Jesus that we have eternal salvation. Jesus is now in heaven preparing a place for all believers.

"_____ _____ _____ _____ _____
_____ _____ _____ _____ _____
_____ _____ _____ _____ _____
_____ _____ _____'_ _____ _____
_____ _____ _____ _____
_____ _____ _____."

A	B	E	F	G	I	L
T	T.	T.	⊥	⊥.	⊥..	⊣

M	O	P	R	T	V	W
⊣.	⊣..	⊢	⊢.	⊢..	▽	▽.

CODE

Wise Men

The Wise Men, or Magi, came from the east to worship Jesus. The Bible doesn't tell us exactly how many of them traveled to see Jesus or what their names were, but they are said to be the first Gentile worshipers of the Christ Child. They presented Him with gifts of gold, frankincense, and myrrh.

Mary Magdalene

Mary Magdalene is mentioned in the Bible more often than any other woman. She was the first person to whom Jesus appeared after His resurrection.

Code

A Y C ⋏ D ⊰ F ⸸ G ⋏ I ⊱ M ⸸
N ⸸ O ⋏ R ⋇ S ⊰ T ⊰ W ⊱ Y ⊱

Mary and Martha

49

Mary and Martha were sisters who opened their home to Jesus and His friends. Mary sat at Jesus' feet, listening to what He said. Martha went about the preparations to feed their guests. When Martha complained to Jesus that Mary wasn't helping her, He replied:

CODE

A △	C ▷	D ◁	E ∧	G >	H <	I ∩
L ⊃	M ⊂	N ⊓	R ⊔	S ⌣	T ⊓	W ⌞

"_ _ _ _ _ _ _ _ _ _ _ _ _ _ _ _

_ _ _ _ _ _ _ _ _ _ _ _ _ _

_ _ _ _ _ _ _ _ _ _ _ _ _ _ _,

_ _ _ _ _ _ _ _ _ _ _ _ _

_ _ _ _ _ _ _ _ _ _ _ _."

Pilate

50

Pontius Pilate was the Roman ruler of Judea. He despised the Jews and their beliefs and only wanted to keep the peace. The Jewish leaders brought Jesus to him for trial. Pilate could find no wrong in Jesus, but he ordered Him crucified because it was what the people wanted.

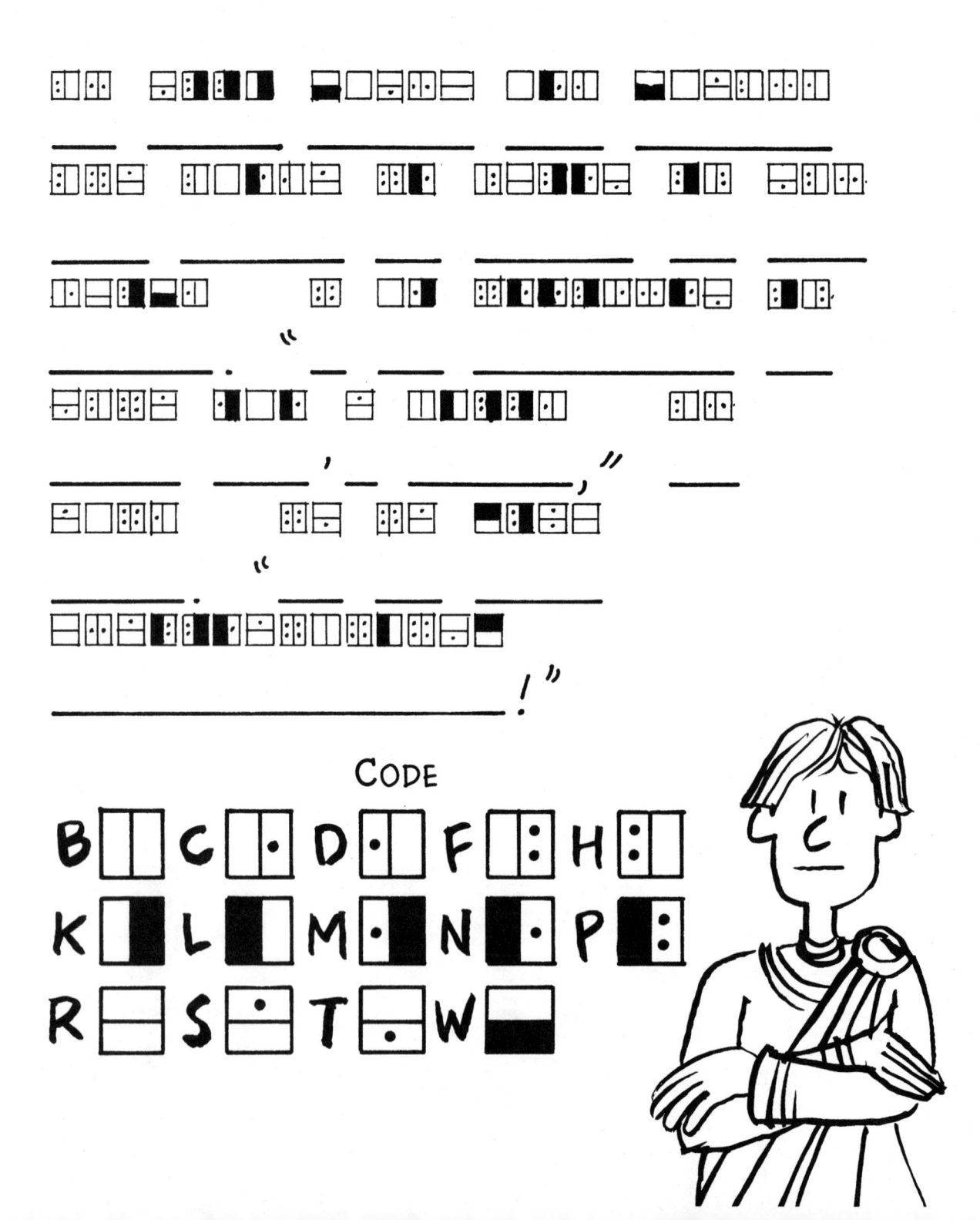

Code

Luke

Luke is referred to as the "beloved physician." Paul calls him his fellow worker for the Lord. Luke is the author of the book that bears his name and also the Acts of the Apostles. Luke's gospel is the most complete and orderly story of the life of Jesus.

51

ΣMWΣM   M   MΣMMW   ΣMΣM   ΣMWM
___ __ _____ ____ ____

WΣMMƵ   MWƵMΣΣMΣMΣMƵ   MƵMWƵ
_____ _____ _____

ΣƵMWΣ   WWWM   ΣƵM   WMΣMWMWΣ
_____ ____ ___ _____ ,

MΣ   ΣMMMMƵ   ΣWWƵ   MMΣW   ΣW
__ _____ ____ ____ __

MM   ΣW   ƵWMΣM   MW   WWƵMWMƵ
__ __ _____ __ _____

MΣΣWΣWΣ   WWW   ƵWΣ
_____ ___ ___ .

CODE

A Ϻ   B W   C Σ   E M

F W   G Σ   I Ϻ   L M   M Ϻ

O W   R W   S Σ   U Σ   W Ƶ

52

Stephen

Stephen, a man full of faith and of the Holy Spirit, was chosen by the disciples to assist in the daily distribution of food. His faith enabled him to do great things among the people. His strong preaching enraged others who eventually stoned him to death. Stephen became the first Christian martyr.

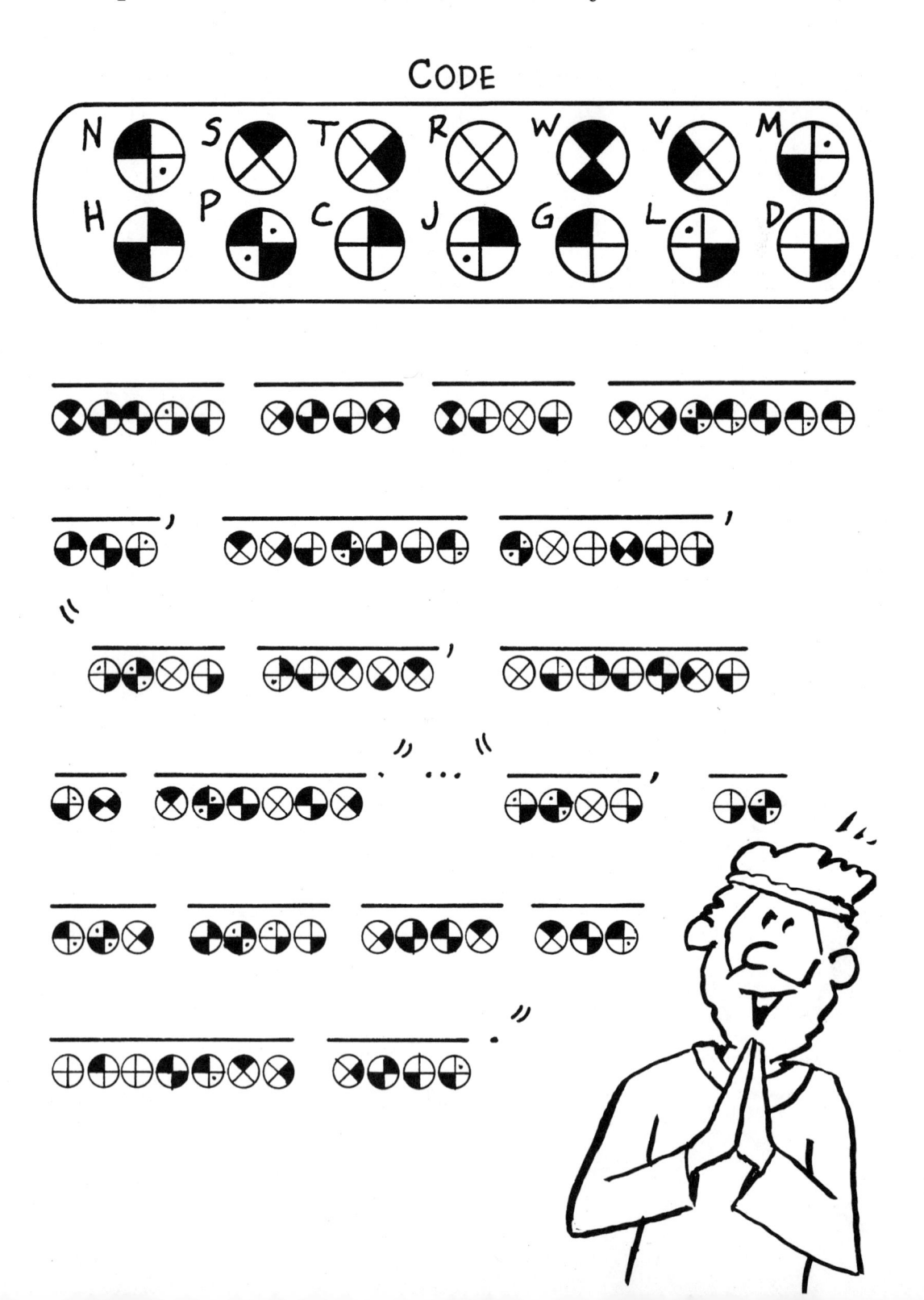

Code

N S T R W V M
H P C J G L D

_____ _____ _____ _____

_____ , _____ _____ ,

" _____ _____ , _____

_____ . . . _____ , _____

_____ _____ _____ _____

_____ _____ . "

Paul

53

Paul's missionary zeal spread the Gospel of Jesus Christ throughout the known world. He helped establish many churches during his missionary journeys. Half of the books in the New Testament were written by Paul. Scriptures depict Paul's personal life as unselfish devotion to the cause of Jesus.

CODE

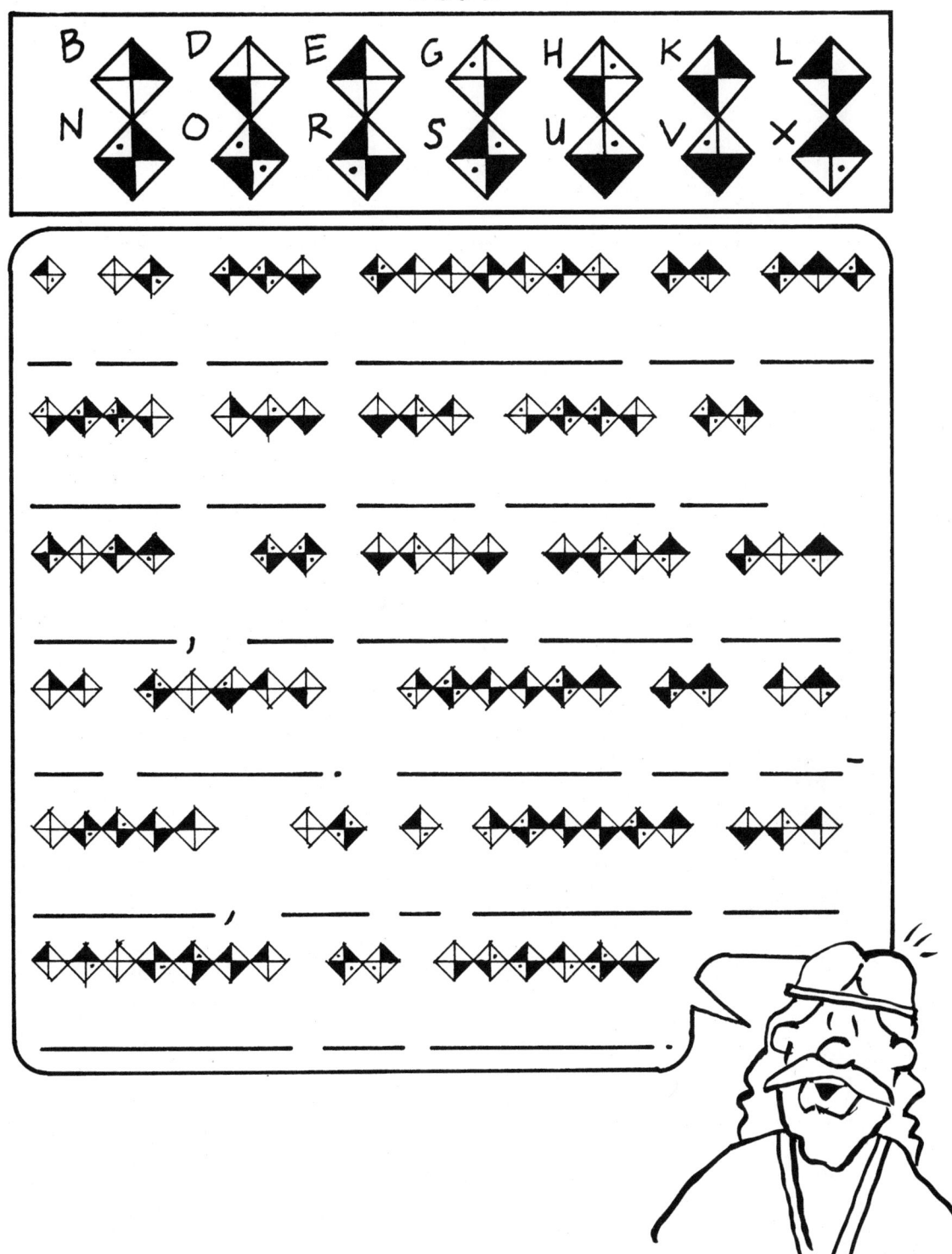

Barnabas

54

Barnabas, which means "son of encouragement," sold some property and gave the money to the apostles to share with others who believed in Christ. It was Barnabas who brought Paul to Antioch, where believers were first called Christians. Barnabas accompanied Paul on his first missionary journey.

THANK YOU, BARNABAS!

Timothy

Timothy learned the Scriptures at an early age from his loving mother and caring grandmother. Paul wrote that Timothy had a gift given him by the laying on of hands by the elders of the church. Timothy became a constant companion of the apostle Paul.

55

__ __ __ __ __ __ __ __ __ __ __ __ __ , __ __ __ __ __ __ __ __
08 09   16 09 26 14   14 17 25 24 14 15 04   08 15 24   17 16   24 12 18

__ __ __ __ __ __ __ __ __ __ __ __ __ ' __ __ __ __ __ __ __
03 18 24 14 15 09 18   01 26 07   13 24 07   16   11 09 23 23 24 08

__ __ __ __ __ __ __ __ __ __ __ __ __ __ __ __ __ __ __ __
08 24 18 21 09 18   17 26   16 22 18 09 01 07 17 26 13   14 15 09

__ __ __ __ __ __ __ __ __ __ __ __ __ __ , __ __ __ __ __ __ __ __ __ __-
13 24 16 22 09 23   24 11   05 15 18 17 16 14   14 24   16 14 18 09 26 13 14 15

__ __ __ __ __ __ __ __ __ __ __ __ __ __
09 26   01 26 07   09 26 05 24 12 18 01 13 09

__ __ __ __ __ __ __ __ __ __ __ __ __ __ .
04 24 12   17 26   04 24 12 18   11 01 17 14 15

CODE
A=01 Z=02 B=03 Y=04

Hi! I'm Timothy!

56 Philemon

Philemon was a leader of the church at Colosse. He had been brought to Christ by Paul. Paul wrote his letter to Philemon to urge him to take back a runaway slave who also had been brought to Christ by Paul. Paul spoke of Philemon as a highly respected Christian.

Answer Key

Old Testament Language—The Messiah is drawing near. Amen.

Adam and Eve—So God created man in His own image, in the image of God He created him; male and female He created them. *Genesis 1:27*

Cain and Abel—But Abel brought fat portions from some of the firstborn of his flock. The Lord looked with favor on Abel and his offering. *Genesis 4:4*

Noah—Noah was a righteous man, blameless among the people of his time, and he walked with God. *Genesis 6:9*

Abraham—"Look up at the heavens and count the stars—if indeed you can count them." Then He said to him, "So shall your offspring be." *Genesis 15:5*

Isaac—"Take your son, your only son, Isaac, whom you love, and go to the region of Moriah. Sacrifice him there as a burnt offering." *Genesis 22:2*

Jacob—"Your name will no longer be Jacob, but Israel, because you have struggled with God and with men and have overcome." *Genesis 32:28*

Joseph—"Listen to this dream I had: We were binding sheaves of grain out in the field when suddenly my sheaf rose and stood upright, while your sheaves gathered around mine and bowed down to it." *Genesis 37:6–7*

Moses—When the Lord finished speaking to Moses on Mount Sinai, He gave him the two tablets of the Testimony, the tablets of stone inscribed by the finger of God. *Exodus 31:18*

Aaron—Make sacred garments for your brother Aaron, to give him dignity and honor. *Exodus 28:2*

Joshua—The Lord gave this command to Joshua son of Nun: "Be strong and courageous, for you will bring the Israelites into the land I promised them on oath, and I Myself will be with you." *Deuteronomy 31:23*

Job—I know that my Redeemer lives, and that in the end He will stand upon the earth. *Job 19:25*

Deborah—"I will go with you. But because of the way you are going about this, the honor will not be yours, for the Lord will hand Sisera over to a woman." *Judges 4:9*

Gideon—Grasping the torches in their left hands and holding in their right hands the trumpets they were to blow, they shouted, "A sword for the Lord and for Gideon!" *Judges 7:20*

Samson—"No razor may be used on his head, because the boy is to be a Nazirite, set apart to God from birth, and he will begin the deliverance of Israel from the hands of the Philistines." *Judges 13:5*

Ruth—"Where you go I will go, and where you stay I will stay. Your people will be my people and your God my God." *Ruth 1:16*

Samuel—"I will teach you the way that is good and right. But be sure to fear the Lord and serve Him faithfully with all your heart." *1 Samuel 12:23–24*

Saul—"You have rejected the word of the Lord, and the Lord has rejected you as king over Israel!" *1 Samuel 15:26*

David—"You come against me with sword and spear and javelin, but I come against you in the name of the Lord Almighty." *1 Samuel 17:45*

Solomon—"So give your servant a discerning heart to govern your people and to distinguish between right and wrong." *1 Kings 3:9*

Elijah—The ravens brought him bread and meat in the morning and bread and meat in the evening, and he drank from the brook. *1 Kings 17:6*

Elisha—"Go, wash yourself seven times in the Jordan, and your flesh will be restored and you will be cleansed." *2 Kings 5:10*

Esther—And these days of Purim should never cease to be celebrated by the Jews, nor should the memory of them die out among their descendants. *Esther 9:28*

Jonah—"But I, with a song of thanksgiving, will sacrifice to You. What I have vowed I will make good. Salvation comes from the Lord." *Jonah 2:9*

Isaiah—For to us a child is born, to us a son is given. … And He will be called Wonderful Counselor, Mighty God, Everlasting Father, Prince of Peace. *Isaiah 9:6*

Jeremiah—"Before I formed you in the womb I knew you, before you were born I set you apart; I appointed you as a prophet to the nations." *Jeremiah 1:5*

Ezekiel—"I will put My spirit in you and you will live, and I will settle you in your own land." *Ezekiel 37:14*

Daniel—"My God sent His angel, and He shut the mouths of the lions. They have not hurt me, because I was found innocent in His sight." *Daniel 6:22*

Shadrach, Meshach, and Abednego—"If we are thrown into the blazing furnace, the God we serve is able to save us from it, and He will rescue us from your hand, O king." *Daniel 3:17*

New Testament Language—Seek the Lord.

Peter—"Who do people say the Son of Man is?" … Simon Peter answered, "You are the Christ, the Son of the Living God." *Matthew 16:13, 16*

Andrew—The first thing Andrew did was to find his brother Simon and tell him, "We have found the Messiah" (that is, the Christ). *John 1:41*

James—James son of Zebedee and his brother John (to them He gave the name Boanerges, which means Sons of Thunder). *Mark 3:17*

John—Dear friends, let us love one another, for love comes from God. Everyone who loves has been born of God and knows God. *1 John 4:7*

Philip—Philip found Nathanael and told him, "We have found the one Moses wrote about in the Law, and about whom the prophets also wrote—Jesus of Nazareth, the son of Joseph." *John 1:45*

Nathanael—When Jesus saw Nathanael approaching, He said of him, "Here is a true Israelite, in whom there is nothing false." *John 1:47*

Thomas—Then he said to Thomas, "Put your finger here; see My hands. Reach out your hand and put it into My side. Stop doubting and believe." *John 20:27*

Matthew—As Jesus went on from there, He saw a man named Matthew sitting at the tax collector's booth. "Follow Me," He told him, and Matthew got up and followed Him. *Matthew 9:9*

Thaddaeus—Then Judas (not Judas Iscariot) said, "But, Lord, why do You intend to show yourself to us and not to the world?" *John 14:22*

Simon—These are the names of the twelve apostles: …Simon the Zealot. *Matthew 10:2, 4*

Judas Iscariot—"I have sinned," he said, "for I have betrayed innocent blood." …So Judas threw the money into the temple and left. Then he went away and hanged himself. *Matthew 27:4–5*

Zechariah—And now you will be silent and not able to speak until the day this happens, because you did not believe My words. *Luke 1:20*

John the Baptist—"I baptize you with water. But one more powerful than I will come, the thongs of whose sandals I am not worthy to untie. He will baptize you with the Holy Spirit and with fire." *Luke 3:16*

Joseph—"Joseph son of David, do not be afraid to take Mary … as your wife, because what is conceived in her is from the Holy Spirit." *Matthew 1:20*

Mary—"Do not be afraid, Mary, you have found favor with God. You will be with child and give birth to a son, and you are to give Him the name Jesus." *Luke 1:30–31*

Jesus Christ—"For God so loved the world that He gave His one and only Son, that whoever believes in Him shall not perish but have eternal life." *John 3:16*

Wise Men—"Where is the one who has been born king of the Jews? We saw His star in the east and have come to worship Him." *Matthew 2:2*

Mary Magdalene—Mary Magdalene went to the disciples with the news: "I have seen the Lord!" And she told them that He had said these things to her. *John 20:18*

Mary and Martha—"But only one thing is needed. Mary has chosen what is better, and it will not be taken away from her." *Luke 10:42*

Pilate—He took water and washed his hands in front of the crowd. "I am innocent of this man's blood," he said. "It is your responsibility!" *Matthew 27:24*

Luke—Since I myself have carefully investigated everything from the beginning, it seemed good also to me to write an orderly account for you. *Luke 1:3*

Stephen—While they were stoning him, Stephen prayed, "Lord Jesus, receive my spirit." … "Lord, do not hold this … against them." *Acts 7:59, 60*

Paul—I am not seeking my own good but the good of many, so that they may be saved. Follow my example, as I follow the example of Christ. *1 Corinthians 10:33–11:1*

Barnabas—He was a good man, full of the Holy Spirit and faith, and a great number of people were brought to the Lord. *Acts 11:24*

Timothy—We sent Timothy, who is our brother and God's fellow worker in spreading the gospel of Christ, to strengthen and encourage you in your faith. *1 Thessalonians 3:2*

Philemon—I always thank my God as I remember you in my prayers, because I hear about your faith in the Lord Jesus and your love for all the saints. *Philemon 4–5*